YOUR LIFE IS A MIRACLE

MIMI NOVIC

Aspiring Hope
Publishing

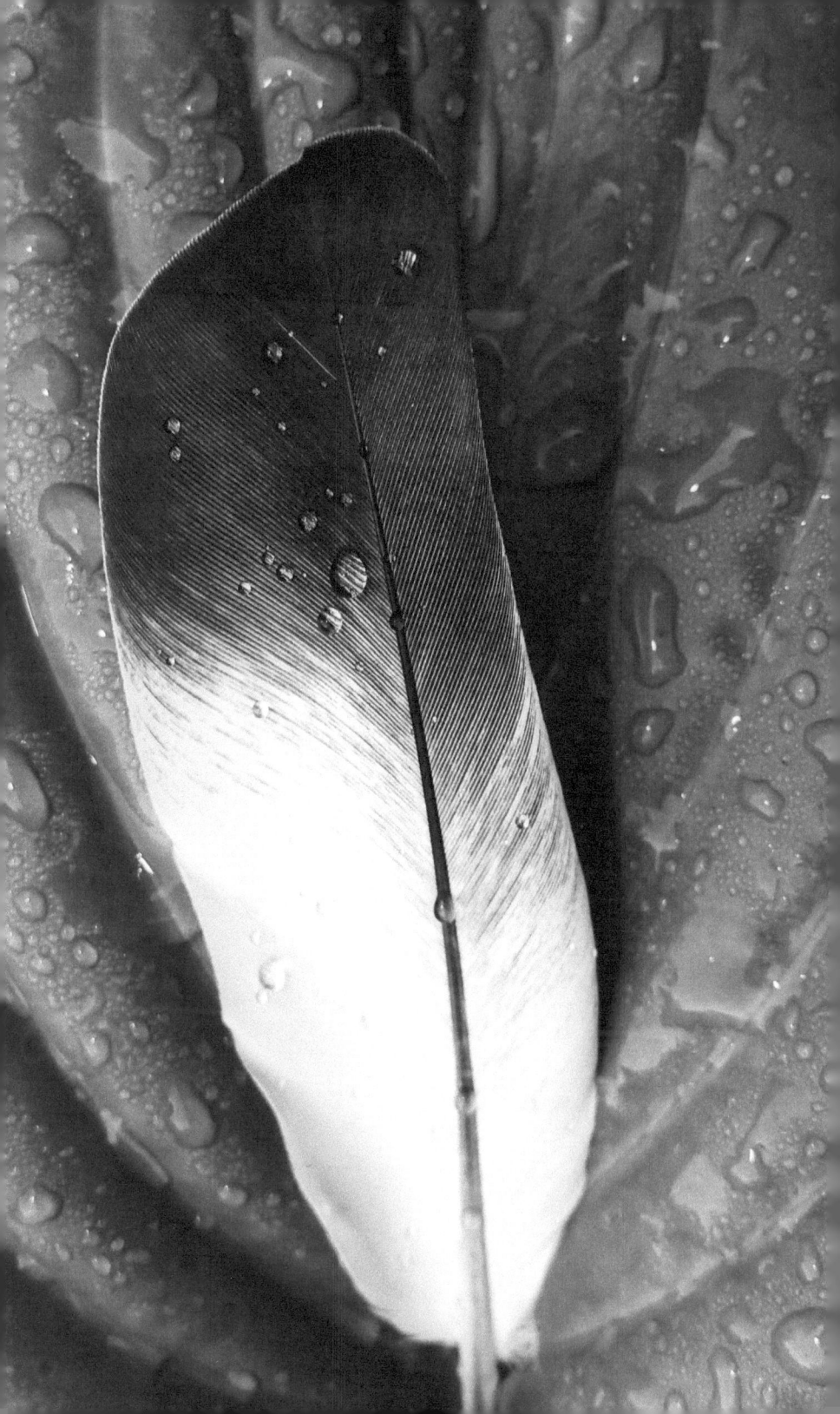

British Library Cataloguing Publication Data.

A Catalogue record for this book is available from the British Library.

ISBN 978-1-9999120-8-6

Published by Aspiring Hope Publishing

Raising funds to support
The Prince's Trust

Prince's Trust

All net proceeds donated to The Prince's Trust.
A registered charity, incorporated by Royal Charter, in England and Wales (1079675) and Scotland (SC041198).

About Mimi Novic

Mimi Novic is one of today's bestselling inspirational authors and is ranked amongst the top names in inspirational, motivational and spiritual books in the world. Her writings and quotes are considered some of the most popular in modern times and are used by some of today's most well known and influential figures.

She is internationally known as one of the most respected and highly regarded motivational and self awareness teachers in the fields of self-development and spiritual growth. Her expertise has made her amongst the most popular and highly demanded well being experts of today.

Working as a complementary medical practitioner, self development teacher, voiceover artist, author and motivational speaker, Mimi has collaborated with some of the most well-known and knowledgeable therapists, composers, musicians, coaches, healers and professionals in their field and bringing together powerful teams that work in synchronicity to bring the best possible life enhancing experiences.

She teaches and runs workshops and seminars in a wide array of therapies, complementary medicine and self-awareness, working around the world in clinics, retreats and on a one to one basis.

For more information about Mimi Novic please visit:

www.miminovic.co.uk

Dear Beautiful Soul

Welcome To A New Beginning.

You are here because you have chosen to embark on a journey that will set you free.

Every step you take along this new road will enlighten you to find your true purpose. Your path becomes a beautiful adventure, full of precious moments, when you are true to the calling of your true being.

As you get closer to knowing yourself, remember this is a sacred place, enjoy with the utmost love and compassion, everything you do.

Use this daily guide to help you find the meaning of your existence and to reach a sense of peace and clarity, where you can dance freely in the light of the higher truth.

We sometimes miss the little reminders that our heart is whispering. We all need a special time for the soul to be our guide and to find a safe oasis where we can find all the answers.
Explore every day with a new zest and embrace it with light, towards inner healing, a more genuine understanding and a celebration of who you are.

May the power and strength you have inside you, be your joy.
Everything begins with you dear soul, and the moment has arrived to change your life.

Wishing you love for the beautiful journey ahead.

When we begin to truly, deeply, love ourselves. The whole world embraces us.

Mimi Novic

How to Use Your Journal

How Do You Feel This Morning:?
Each morning when you wake up become aware of how you are feeling, what thoughts come to your mind, and slowly allow yourself to express those words on paper. This is a way to become more in tune with your feelings and gradually they will become easier to process.

What Would You Like To Achieve Today?
Set your intentions for the day focusing on your goals, aims and what you want to embrace.

Accomplishment Aim For The Day:
Go through and complete the task of the day which will help you gain insight and self awareness through the process of mindful activities.

How Will You Show Yourself Kindness Today?
Write a list of self-care practices that you will do for yourself and complete them during the day to highlight the importance of compassion towards yourself.

Reflections Of The Day:
Write one sentence to describe how the day went.

What Did You Achieve Today?
Keep a record of your daily achievements and insights, this will help you celebrate completed tasks.

How Do You Feel This Evening?
Express your feelings freely and how you feel about yourself, the people you interacted with, what made you happy, sad and hopeful.

What Could Have Been Better Today?
Reflect on areas for improvement without self-criticism, focusing on your growth and learning.

Positive Thought Of The Day & Looking Forward:
Consider what you experienced throughout the day and evening and write one line to express something positive that you learnt and what you are looking forward to.

Quote of the Day

We may meet many people along this long road, but it is of no use,
Until we finally meet ourselves.
Mimi Novic

Good Morning Beautiful Soul!

How Do You Feel This Morning?

_____

_____

_____

What Would You Like To Achieve Today?

_____

_____

_____

Accomplishment Aim For The Day:

Slowly throughout the day become aware of how much time you are spending on your computer, and other electronic devices. Notice how your body and mind respond to the digital noise. Begin every day to spend one hour less on your devices and document at the end of each day how you feel. Write about the experience.

_____

_____

_____

How Will You Show Yourself Kindness Today?

_____

_____

_____

Good Evening Beautiful One

Reflections Of The Day

_____

_____

_____

What Did You Achieve Today?

_____

_____

_____

How Do You Feel This Evening?

_____

_____

_____

What Could Have Been Better Today?

_____

_____

_____

Positive Thought Of The Day & Looking Forward

_____

_____

_____

Notes & Reminders

Quote of the Day

Laughter is the language of the soul.
Pablo Neruda

Good Morning Beautiful Soul!

How Do You Feel This Morning?

_____

_____

_____

What Would You Like To Achieve Today?

_____

_____

_____

Accomplishment Aim For The Day:

Meditation Exploration: Spend time researching and journaling about various forms of meditation that you would like to try. Choose one that you can do daily and make notes how it makes you feel.

_____

_____

_____

How Will You Show Yourself Kindness Today?

_____

_____

_____

Good Evening Beautiful One

Reflections Of The Day

_____
_____
_____

What Did You Achieve Today?

_____
_____
_____

How Do You Feel This Evening?

_____
_____
_____

What Could Have Been Better Today?

_____
_____
_____

Positive Thought Of The Day & Looking Forward

_____
_____
_____

Notes & Reminders

Quote of the Day

Yesterday I was clever, so I wanted to change the world.
Today I am wise, so I am changing myself.
Rumi

Good Morning Beautiful Soul!

How Do You Feel This Morning?

_____
_____
_____

What Would You Like To Achieve Today?

_____
_____
_____

Accomplishment Aim For The Day:

Affirmations: Write three affirmations that you can say to yourself every day for forty days. Make it a personal and positive statement. Write down what each of them mean to you.

_____
_____
_____
_____

How Will You Show Yourself Kindness Today?

_____
_____
_____

Good Evening Beautiful One

Reflections Of The Day

_____

_____

_____

What Did You Achieve Today?

_____

_____

_____

How Do You Feel This Evening?

_____

_____

_____

What Could Have Been Better Today?

_____

_____

_____

Positive Thought Of The Day & Looking Forward

_____

_____

_____

Notes & Reminders

Quote of the Day

Out of suffering have emerged the strongest souls; the most massive characters are
seared with scars.
Kahlil Gibran

Good Morning Beautiful Soul!

How Do You Feel This Morning?

What Would You Like To Achieve Today?

Accomplishment Aim For The Day:

Inspirational Speaker: Listen to a talk by an inspirational speaker and journal about the
insights and inspirations you gain. Think and write about what talk you would give if you
had the chance to give a speech.

How Will You Show Yourself Kindness Today?

Good Evening Beautiful One

Reflections Of The Day

_____

_____

_____

What Did You Achieve Today?

_____

_____

_____

How Do You Feel This Evening?

_____

_____

_____

What Could Have Been Better Today?

_____

_____

_____

Positive Thought Of The Day & Looking Forward

_____

_____

_____

Notes & Reminders

Quote of the Day

Remember that wherever your heart is,
There you will find your treasure.
Paulo Coelho

Good Morning Beautiful Soul!

How Do You Feel This Morning?

_____
_____
_____

What Would You Like To Achieve Today?

_____
_____
_____

Accomplishment Aim For The Day:

Sky Gazing: Each morning when you wake up, look at the morning sky and write down three emotions you're feeling. Each evening look at the night sky and write three emotions that you feel.

_____
_____
_____

How Will You Show Yourself Kindness Today?

_____
_____
_____

Good Evening Beautiful One

Reflections Of The Day

_____
_____
_____

What Did You Achieve Today?

_____
_____
_____

How Do You Feel This Evening?

_____
_____
_____

What Could Have Been Better Today?

_____
_____
_____

Positive Thought Of The Day & Looking Forward

_____
_____
_____

Notes & Reminders

Quote of the Day

I wish I could show you when you are lonely or in darkness the astonishing light of your own being.
Hafiz

Good Morning Beautiful Soul!

How Do You Feel This Morning?

_____

_____

_____

What Would You Like To Achieve Today?

_____

_____

_____

Accomplishment Aim For The Day:

Aromatherapy: Explore the power of aromatherapy and it's benefits. Read and learn about diffusing, making use of calming or energizing essential oil blends. Write down which appeal to you and how you see them helping you.

_____

_____

_____

How Will You Show Yourself Kindness Today?

_____

_____

_____

Good Evening Beautiful One

Reflections Of The Day

_____
_____
_____

What Did You Achieve Today?

_____
_____
_____

How Do You Feel This Evening?

_____
_____
_____

What Could Have Been Better Today?

_____
_____
_____

Positive Thought Of The Day & Looking Forward

_____
_____
_____

Notes & Reminders

Quote of the Day

For nothing will be impossible with God.
Luke 1:37

Good Morning Beautiful Soul!

How Do You Feel This Morning?

What Would You Like To Achieve Today?

Accomplishment Aim For The Day:

Finding Beauty: Start looking around you and see what you find beautiful. Take some photographs of what inspires you and makes you feel good. Write down the feelings you feel when you look at these things.

How Will You Show Yourself Kindness Today?

Good Evening Beautiful One

Reflections Of The Day

_____

_____

_____

What Did You Achieve Today?

_____

_____

_____

How Do You Feel This Evening?

_____

_____

_____

What Could Have Been Better Today?

_____

_____

_____

Positive Thought Of The Day & Looking Forward

_____

_____

_____

Notes & Reminders

We are what we believe we are.
C.S.Lewis

Good Morning Beautiful Soul!

How Do You Feel This Morning?

_____

_____

_____

What Would You Like To Achieve Today?

_____

_____

_____

Accomplishment Aim For The Day:

Energising Or Relaxing Shower/Bath: Enjoy a bath or shower using your favourite blends of oils, and any other soothing ingredients. Write down how you feel afterwards.

_____

_____

_____

How Will You Show Yourself Kindness Today?

_____

_____

_____

Good Evening Beautiful One

Reflections Of The Day

_____

_____

_____

What Did You Achieve Today?

_____

_____

_____

How Do You Feel This Evening?

_____

_____

_____

What Could Have Been Better Today?

_____

_____

_____

Positive Thought Of The Day & Looking Forward

_____

_____

_____

Notes & Reminders

Quote of the Day

Music expresses that which cannot be put into words and that which cannot remain silent.
Victor Hugo

Good Morning Beautiful Soul!

How Do You Feel This Morning?

_____

_____

_____

What Would You Like To Achieve Today?

_____

_____

_____

Accomplishment Aim For The Day:

Nature Photography: Take a camera or your phone and capture the beauty of nature through photography. Write down how being in nature makes you feel.

_____

_____

_____

How Will You Show Yourself Kindness Today?

_____

_____

_____

Good Evening Beautiful One

Reflections Of The Day

_____
_____
_____

What Did You Achieve Today?

_____
_____
_____

How Do You Feel This Evening?

_____
_____
_____

What Could Have Been Better Today?

_____
_____
_____

Positive Thought Of The Day & Looking Forward

_____
_____
_____

Notes & Reminders

Quote of the Day

I am the drop that contains the ocean.
Yunus Emre

Good Morning Beautiful Soul!

How Do You Feel This Morning?

_____
_____
_____

What Would You Like To Achieve Today?

_____
_____
_____

Accomplishment Aim For The Day:

Colour Therapy: Spend the day wearing your favourite colour or decorating a space in that colour. Reflect on how colours influence your mood.

_____
_____
_____

How Will You Show Yourself Kindness Today?

_____
_____
_____

Good Evening Beautiful One

Reflections Of The Day

_____
_____
_____

What Did You Achieve Today?

_____
_____
_____

How Do You Feel This Evening?

_____
_____
_____

What Could Have Been Better Today?

_____
_____
_____

Positive Thought Of The Day & Looking Forward

_____
_____
_____

Notes & Reminders

Quote of the Day

The true man attaches his heart to none but God.
Bayazid Bastami

Good Morning Beautiful Soul!

How Do You Feel This Morning?

_____

_____

_____

What Would You Like To Achieve Today?

_____

_____

_____

Accomplishment Aim For The Day:

Podcast Exploration: Find and listen to a podcast on a topic you know nothing about but would like to learn more. Write down the podcast name and explore what you learnt.

_____

_____

_____

How Will You Show Yourself Kindness Today?

_____

_____

_____

Good Evening Beautiful One

Reflections Of The Day

_____
_____
_____

What Did You Achieve Today?

_____
_____
_____

How Do You Feel This Evening?

_____
_____
_____

What Could Have Been Better Today?

_____
_____
_____

Positive Thought Of The Day & Looking Forward

_____
_____
_____

Notes & Reminders

Quote of the Day

For prayer is nothing else than being on terms of friendship with God.
Teresa of Ávila

Good Morning Beautiful Soul!

How Do You Feel This Morning?

_____

_____

_____

What Would You Like To Achieve Today?

_____

_____

_____

Accomplishment Aim For The Day:

Quote Making: Make up five quotes on inspiration and motivation that you feel would benefit others.

_____

_____

_____

How Will You Show Yourself Kindness Today?

_____

_____

_____

Good Evening Beautiful One

Reflections Of The Day

_____
_____
_____

What Did You Achieve Today?

_____
_____
_____

How Do You Feel This Evening?

_____
_____

What Could Have Been Better Today?

_____
_____
_____

Positive Thought Of The Day & Looking Forward

_____
_____
_____

Notes & Reminders

Quote of the Day

Nothing is forever except change.
Buddha

Good Morning Beautiful Soul!

How Do You Feel This Morning?

What Would You Like To Achieve Today?

Accomplishment Aim For The Day:

Future Goals: Spend time visualising your goals in detail, focusing on how you plan to achieve them. Write down five goals you're ready to start working on.

How Will You Show Yourself Kindness Today?

Good Evening Beautiful One

Reflections Of The Day

_____
_____
_____

What Did You Achieve Today?

_____
_____
_____

How Do You Feel This Evening?

_____
_____
_____

What Could Have Been Better Today?

_____
_____
_____

Positive Thought Of The Day & Looking Forward

_____
_____
_____

Notes & Reminders

Quote of the Day

It does not matter how slowly you go as long as you do not stop.
Confucius

Good Morning Beautiful Soul!

How Do You Feel This Morning?

What Would You Like To Achieve Today?

Accomplishment Aim For The Day:

Voice Journaling: Spend some time voice journaling, speaking your thoughts and feelings aloud and recording them. Write down how you feel as you speak your truth.

How Will You Show Yourself Kindness Today?

Good Evening Beautiful One

Reflections Of The Day

_____

_____

_____

What Did You Achieve Today?

_____

_____

_____

How Do You Feel This Evening?

_____

_____

_____

What Could Have Been Better Today?

_____

_____

_____

Positive Thought Of The Day & Looking Forward

_____

_____

_____

Notes & Reminders

Quote of the Day

Everyone thinks of changing the world, but no one thinks of changing himself.
Leo Tolstoy

Good Morning Beautiful Soul!

How Do You Feel This Morning?

What Would You Like To Achieve Today?

Accomplishment Aim For The Day:

Kitchen Experiment: Experiment with creating a new dish without following a recipe. Enjoy the process of creativity and improvisation. Write the recipe down and how you felt afterwards when you finished the meal.

How Will You Show Yourself Kindness Today?

Good Evening Beautiful One

Reflections Of The Day

_____
_____
_____

What Did You Achieve Today?

_____
_____
_____

How Do You Feel This Evening?

_____
_____
_____

What Could Have Been Better Today?

_____
_____
_____

Positive Thought Of The Day & Looking Forward

_____
_____
_____

Notes & Reminders

Quote of the Day

I am not what happened to me, I am what I choose to become.
Carl Gustav Jung

Good Morning Beautiful Soul!

How Do You Feel This Morning?

_____

_____

_____

What Would You Like To Achieve Today?

_____

_____

_____

Accomplishment Aim For The Day:

Act of Self-Love: Do five things for yourself that make you feel love for yourself. Write them down.

_____

_____

_____

How Will You Show Yourself Kindness Today?

_____

_____

_____

Good Evening Beautiful One

Reflections Of The Day

_____

_____

_____

What Did You Achieve Today?

_____

_____

_____

How Do You Feel This Evening?

_____

_____

What Could Have Been Better Today?

_____

_____

_____

Positive Thought Of The Day & Looking Forward

_____

_____

_____

Notes & Reminders

Quote of the Day

Your only obligation in any lifetime is to be true to yourself.
Richard Bach

Good Morning Beautiful Soul!

How Do You Feel This Morning?

_____

_____

_____

What Would You Like To Achieve Today?

_____

_____

_____

Accomplishment Aim For The Day:

Explore a New Genre: Listen to some music and watch a movie in a genre you've never tried. Reflect on the experience.

_____

_____

_____

How Will You Show Yourself Kindness Today?

_____

_____

_____

Good Evening Beautiful One

Reflections Of The Day

_____

_____

_____

What Did You Achieve Today?

_____

_____

_____

How Do You Feel This Evening?

_____

_____

_____

What Could Have Been Better Today?

_____

_____

_____

Positive Thought Of The Day & Looking Forward

_____

_____

_____

Notes & Reminders

DATE: _____

Quote of the Day

We must accept finite disappointment but never lose infinite hope.
Martin Luther King Jr

Good Morning Beautiful Soul!

How Do You Feel This Morning?

_____
_____

What Would You Like To Achieve Today?

_____
_____

Accomplishment Aim For The Day:

Mindful Breathing: Find a breathing exercise that you feel comfortable with. Begin to do this exercise for forty days and note the effects.

_____
_____

How Will You Show Yourself Kindness Today?

_____
_____

Good Evening Beautiful One

Reflections Of The Day

_____

_____

_____

What Did You Achieve Today?

_____

_____

_____

How Do You Feel This Evening?

_____

_____

_____

What Could Have Been Better Today?

_____

_____

_____

Positive Thought Of The Day & Looking Forward

_____

_____

_____

Notes & Reminders

Quote of the Day

Life is the dancer and you are the dance.
Eckhart Tolle

Good Morning Beautiful Soul!

How Do You Feel This Morning?

_____

_____

_____

What Would You Like To Achieve Today?

_____

_____

_____

Accomplishment Aim For The Day:

Remember Your Success: Think about five things that you are proud of that you have achieved in your life so far. Write them down and how they made you feel.

_____

_____

_____

How Will You Show Yourself Kindness Today?

_____

_____

_____

Good Evening Beautiful One

Reflections Of The Day

_____
_____
_____

What Did You Achieve Today?

_____
_____
_____

How Do You Feel This Evening?

_____
_____
_____

What Could Have Been Better Today?

_____
_____
_____

Positive Thought Of The Day & Looking Forward

_____
_____
_____

Notes & Reminders

Quote of the Day

The only true wisdom is in knowing you know nothing.
Socrates

Good Morning Beautiful Soul!

How Do You Feel This Morning?

_____

_____

_____

What Would You Like To Achieve Today?

_____

_____

_____

Accomplishment Aim For The Day:

Choose Your Mood: Choose three different pieces of your favourite music or songs and write them down and what mood it puts you in. Be detailed in your reply.

_____

_____

_____

How Will You Show Yourself Kindness Today?

_____

_____

_____

Good Evening Beautiful One

Reflections Of The Day

_____

_____

_____

What Did You Achieve Today?

_____

_____

_____

How Do You Feel This Evening?

_____

_____

_____

What Could Have Been Better Today?

_____

_____

_____

Positive Thought Of The Day & Looking Forward

_____

_____

_____

Notes & Reminders

Quote of the Day

The mystery of human existence lies not in just staying alive, but in finding something to live for.
Fyodor Dostoyevsky

Good Morning Beautiful Soul!

How Do You Feel This Morning?

_____

_____

_____

What Would You Like To Achieve Today?

_____

_____

_____

Accomplishment Aim For The Day:

Inspirational People: Think about who inspires you. Write down five people who inspire you and why. They can be people you know or people you would like to meet.

_____

_____

_____

How Will You Show Yourself Kindness Today?

_____

_____

_____

Good Evening Beautiful One

Reflections Of The Day

_____
_____
_____

What Did You Achieve Today?

_____
_____
_____

How Do You Feel This Evening?

_____
_____
_____

What Could Have Been Better Today?

_____
_____
_____

Positive Thought Of The Day & Looking Forward

_____
_____
_____

Notes & Reminders

Quote of the Day

To be yourself in a world that is constantly trying to make you something else is the greatest accomplishment.
Ralph Waldo Emerson

Good Morning Beautiful Soul!

How Do You Feel This Morning?

_____

_____

_____

What Would You Like To Achieve Today?

_____

_____

_____

Accomplishment Aim For The Day:

Favourite Things List: Make a list of your favourite things across different categories Books, Films, Songs, Food.

_____

_____

_____

How Will You Show Yourself Kindness Today?

_____

_____

_____

Good Evening Beautiful One

Reflections Of The Day

_____
_____
_____

What Did You Achieve Today?

_____
_____
_____

How Do You Feel This Evening?

_____
_____
_____

What Could Have Been Better Today?

_____
_____
_____

Positive Thought Of The Day & Looking Forward

_____
_____
_____

Notes & Reminders

Quote of the Day

What doesn't hurt is not life; what doesn't pass is not happiness.
Ivo Andric

Good Morning Beautiful Soul!

How Do You Feel This Morning?

_____

_____

_____

What Would You Like To Achieve Today?

_____

_____

_____

Accomplishment Aim For The Day:

Positivity About Yourself: Write five positive things about yourself and place them where you'll see them throughout the day.

_____

_____

_____

How Will You Show Yourself Kindness Today?

_____

_____

_____

Good Evening Beautiful One

Reflections Of The Day

_____
_____
_____

What Did You Achieve Today?

_____
_____
_____

How Do You Feel This Evening?

_____
_____
_____

What Could Have Been Better Today?

_____
_____
_____

Positive Thought Of The Day & Looking Forward

_____
_____
_____

Notes & Reminders

Quote of the Day

And now here is my secret, a very simple secret: It is only with the heart that one can see rightly; what is essential is invisible to the eye.
Antoine de Saint-Exupéry,

Good Morning Beautiful Soul!

How Do You Feel This Morning?

_____
_____
_____

What Would You Like To Achieve Today?

_____
_____
_____

Accomplishment Aim For The Day:

Places To Visit: Think about the places you would like to visit in the world and write a list of the destinations and why you would like to go there.

_____
_____
_____

How Will You Show Yourself Kindness Today?

_____
_____
_____

Good Evening Beautiful One

Reflections Of The Day

_____

_____

_____

What Did You Achieve Today?

_____

_____

_____

How Do You Feel This Evening?

_____

_____

_____

What Could Have Been Better Today?

_____

_____

_____

Positive Thought Of The Day & Looking Forward

_____

_____

_____

Notes & Reminders

Quote of the Day

It's not because things are difficult that we do not dare, it is because we do not dare that things are difficult.
Seneca

Good Morning Beautiful Soul!

How Do You Feel This Morning?

_____

_____

_____

What Would You Like To Achieve Today?

_____

_____

_____

Accomplishment Aim For The Day:

Beautiful Memories: Reflect on specific memories and experiences in your life that made you feel happy and content. Write them down in detail.

_____

_____

_____

How Will You Show Yourself Kindness Today?

_____

_____

_____

Good Evening Beautiful One

Reflections Of The Day

_____

_____

_____

What Did You Achieve Today?

_____

_____

_____

How Do You Feel This Evening?

_____

_____

_____

What Could Have Been Better Today?

_____

_____

_____

Positive Thought Of The Day & Looking Forward

_____

_____

_____

Notes & Reminders

Quote of the Day

Imagination is more important than knowledge.
Albert Einstein

Good Morning Beautiful Soul!

How Do You Feel This Morning?

What Would You Like To Achieve Today?

Accomplishment Aim For The Day:

.

Handwritten Letters: Choose five people you will write a handwritten letter to expressing how you feel about them. Write the letters with honesty but don't send them. Note how you feel after writing each letter.

How Will You Show Yourself Kindness Today?

Good Evening Beautiful One

Reflections Of The Day

_____
_____
_____

What Did You Achieve Today?

_____
_____
_____

How Do You Feel This Evening?

_____
_____
_____

What Could Have Been Better Today?

_____
_____
_____

Positive Thought Of The Day & Looking Forward

_____
_____
_____

Notes & Reminders

Quote of the Day

Education is the most powerful weapon which you can use to change the world.
Nelson Mandela

Good Morning Beautiful Soul!

How Do You Feel This Morning?

_____

_____

_____

What Would You Like To Achieve Today?

_____

_____

_____

Accomplishment Aim For The Day:

Seven Day Food Diary: Look into your eating habits for a week. Write down each day what you eat and where you feel you can improve your diet to make it more healthy and nutritious.

_____

_____

_____

How Will You Show Yourself Kindness Today?

_____

_____

_____

Good Evening Beautiful One

Reflections Of The Day

_____

_____

_____

What Did You Achieve Today?

_____

_____

_____

How Do You Feel This Evening?

_____

_____

_____

What Could Have Been Better Today?

_____

_____

_____

Positive Thought Of The Day & Looking Forward

_____

_____

_____

Notes & Reminders

Quote of the Day

We don't see things as they are
We see things as we are.
Anais Nin

Good Morning Beautiful Soul!

How Do You Feel This Morning?

_____
_____
_____

What Would You Like To Achieve Today?

_____
_____
_____

Accomplishment Aim For The Day:

Letter To Your Heart: Write a letter to your heart. Tell it your dreams, what makes you sad, what makes you happy. Be free in your writing and write with love and compassion.

_____
_____
_____

How Will You Show Yourself Kindness Today?

_____
_____
_____

Good Evening Beautiful One

Reflections Of The Day

_____

_____

_____

What Did You Achieve Today?

_____

_____

_____

How Do You Feel This Evening?

_____

_____

_____

What Could Have Been Better Today?

_____

_____

_____

Positive Thought Of The Day & Looking Forward

_____

_____

_____

Notes & Reminders

Quote of the Day

Until you value yourself, you won't value your time. Until you value your time, you will
not do anything with it.
M.Scott Peck

Good Morning Beautiful Soul!

How Do You Feel This Morning?

_____

_____

_____

What Would You Like To Achieve Today?

_____

_____

_____

Accomplishment Aim For The Day:

Let Go Of Your Fears: Write down five of your fears and consider practical steps you are
going to take to conquer them.

_____

_____

_____

How Will You Show Yourself Kindness Today?

_____

_____

_____

Good Evening Beautiful One

Reflections Of The Day

_____
_____
_____

What Did You Achieve Today?

_____
_____
_____

How Do You Feel This Evening?

_____
_____
_____

What Could Have Been Better Today?

_____
_____
_____

Positive Thought Of The Day & Looking Forward

_____
_____
_____

Notes & Reminders

Quote of the Day

Life is either a daring adventure or nothing at all.
Helen Keller

Good Morning Beautiful Soul!

How Do You Feel This Morning?

_____
_____
_____

What Would You Like To Achieve Today?

_____
_____
_____

Accomplishment Aim For The Day:

Explore Your Country: Be a tourist in your own country and visit a place you've never been to. Write about the adventure.

_____
_____
_____

How Will You Show Yourself Kindness Today?

_____
_____
_____

Good Evening Beautiful One

Reflections Of The Day

_____

_____

_____

What Did You Achieve Today?

_____

_____

_____

How Do You Feel This Evening?

_____

_____

_____

What Could Have Been Better Today?

_____

_____

_____

Positive Thought Of The Day & Looking Forward

_____

_____

_____

Notes & Reminders

Quote of the Day

Enlightenment means taking full responsibility for your life.
William Blake

Good Morning Beautiful Soul!

How Do You Feel This Morning?

_____

_____

_____

What Would You Like To Achieve Today?

_____

_____

_____

Accomplishment Aim For The Day:

Forgiveness Letter: Write a letter of forgiveness to someone who you feel has hurt you.
You don't have to send it. Reflect on the feelings of letting go.

_____

_____

_____

How Will You Show Yourself Kindness Today?

_____

_____

_____

Good Evening Beautiful One

Reflections Of The Day

_____
_____
_____

What Did You Achieve Today?

_____
_____
_____

How Do You Feel This Evening?

_____
_____
_____

What Could Have Been Better Today?

_____
_____
_____

Positive Thought Of The Day & Looking Forward

_____
_____
_____

Notes & Reminders

Quote of the Day

Knowing yourself is the beginning of all wisdom.
Aristotle

Good Morning Beautiful Soul!

How Do You Feel This Morning?

What Would You Like To Achieve Today?

Accomplishment Aim For The Day:

What Really Matters To You: Think about what really matters to you in your life. Write about this honestly and openly.

How Will You Show Yourself Kindness Today?

Good Evening Beautiful One

Reflections Of The Day

_____
_____
_____

What Did You Achieve Today?

_____
_____
_____

How Do You Feel This Evening?

_____
_____
_____

What Could Have Been Better Today?

_____
_____
_____

Positive Thought Of The Day & Looking Forward

_____
_____
_____

Notes & Reminders

Quote of the Day

May you live all the days of your life.
Jonathan Swift

Good Morning Beautiful Soul!

How Do You Feel This Morning?

_____
_____
_____

What Would You Like To Achieve Today?

_____
_____
_____

Accomplishment Aim For The Day:

Younger Self: Write a letter to your younger self. Share your life experiences to date and what successes you have achieved and what you have learnt along the way.

_____
_____
_____

How Will You Show Yourself Kindness Today?

_____
_____
_____

Good Evening Beautiful One

Reflections Of The Day

_____

_____

_____

What Did You Achieve Today?

_____

_____

_____

How Do You Feel This Evening?

_____

_____

_____

What Could Have Been Better Today?

_____

_____

_____

Positive Thought Of The Day & Looking Forward

_____

_____

_____

Notes & Reminders

DATE:

What would life be if we had no courage to attempt anything
Vincent Van Gogh

Good Morning Beautiful Soul!

How Do You Feel This Morning?

_____

_____

_____

What Would You Like To Achieve Today?

_____

_____

_____

Accomplishment Aim For The Day:

Words Of Kindness: Tell five people today something kind. Watch their reaction and make notes on how it makes you feel.

_____

_____

_____

How Will You Show Yourself Kindness Today?

_____

_____

_____

Good Evening Beautiful One

Reflections Of The Day

_____

_____

_____

What Did You Achieve Today?

_____

_____

_____

How Do You Feel This Evening?

_____

_____

_____

What Could Have Been Better Today?

_____

_____

_____

Positive Thought Of The Day & Looking Forward

_____

_____

_____

Notes & Reminders

DATE:

Good Morning Beautiful Soul!

How Do You Feel This Morning?

_____
_____
_____

What Would You Like To Achieve Today?

_____
_____
_____

Accomplishment Aim For The Day:

Write a Short Story: Let your imagination be free and write a stoey with you as the main character.

_____
_____
_____

How Will You Show Yourself Kindness Today?

_____
_____
_____

Good Evening Beautiful One

Reflections Of The Day

_____
_____
_____

What Did You Achieve Today?

_____
_____
_____

How Do You Feel This Evening?

_____
_____
_____

What Could Have Been Better Today?

_____
_____
_____

Positive Thought Of The Day & Looking Forward

_____
_____
_____

Notes & Reminders

Quote of the Day

Faith consists in believing when it is beyond the power of reason to believe.
Voltaire

Good Morning Beautiful Soul!

How Do You Feel This Morning?

_____
_____
_____

What Would You Like To Achieve Today?

_____
_____
_____

Accomplishment Aim For The Day:

Guided Meditation: Choose a guided meditation that you've never tried before. See how it makes you feel and what benefits it brings. Write about the experience.

_____
_____
_____

How Will You Show Yourself Kindness Today?

_____
_____
_____

Good Evening Beautiful One

Reflections Of The Day

_____
_____
_____

What Did You Achieve Today?

_____
_____
_____

How Do You Feel This Evening?

_____
_____
_____

What Could Have Been Better Today?

_____
_____
_____

Positive Thought Of The Day & Looking Forward

_____
_____
_____

Notes & Reminders

Quote of the Day

To be beautiful means to be yourself. You don't need to be accepted by others. You need to accept yourself.
Thich Nhat Hanh

Good Morning Beautiful Soul!

How Do You Feel This Morning?

_____

_____

_____

What Would You Like To Achieve Today?

_____

_____

_____

Accomplishment Aim For The Day:

Artistic Moments: Take five photos that bring you joy and write a quote to go with the image about anything that inspires you.

_____

_____

_____

How Will You Show Yourself Kindness Today?

_____

_____

_____

Good Evening Beautiful One

Reflections Of The Day

_____
_____
_____

What Did You Achieve Today?

_____
_____
_____

How Do You Feel This Evening?

_____
_____
_____

What Could Have Been Better Today?

_____
_____
_____

Positive Thought Of The Day & Looking Forward

_____
_____
_____

Notes & Reminders

Quote of the Day

We are all in the gutter, but some of us are looking at the stars.
Oscar Wilde

Good Morning Beautiful Soul!

How Do You Feel This Morning?

What Would You Like To Achieve Today?

Accomplishment Aim For The Day:

Discover Culture: Choose three videos about different cultures around the world that interest you. Write about each of them and how they make you feel.

How Will You Show Yourself Kindness Today?

Good Evening Beautiful One

Reflections Of The Day

_____

_____

_____

What Did You Achieve Today?

_____

_____

_____

How Do You Feel This Evening?

_____

_____

_____

What Could Have Been Better Today?

_____

_____

_____

Positive Thought Of The Day & Looking Forward

_____

_____

_____

Notes & Reminders

Quote of the Day

The greatest wealth is to live content with little.
Plato

Good Morning Beautiful Soul!

How Do You Feel This Morning?

_____

_____

_____

What Would You Like To Achieve Today?

_____

_____

_____

Accomplishment Aim For The Day:

Today Is Your Day: Choose a day and time in the week where you do something relaxing and enjoyable for yourself. Write down what you did and how it felt.

_____

_____

_____

How Will You Show Yourself Kindness Today?

_____

_____

_____

Good Evening Beautiful One

Reflections Of The Day

_____

_____

_____

What Did You Achieve Today?

_____

_____

_____

How Do You Feel This Evening?

_____

_____

_____

What Could Have Been Better Today?

_____

_____

_____

Positive Thought Of The Day & Looking Forward

_____

_____

_____

Notes & Reminders

Quote of the Day

If you have the ability to love, love yourself first.
Charles Bukowski

Good Morning Beautiful Soul!

How Do You Feel This Morning?

What Would You Like To Achieve Today?

Accomplishment Aim For The Day:

Gratitude Jar: Start a gratitude jar, writing down five things you're grateful for each day.

How Will You Show Yourself Kindness Today?

Good Evening Beautiful One

Reflections Of The Day

_____
_____
_____

What Did You Achieve Today?

_____
_____
_____

How Do You Feel This Evening?

_____
_____
_____

What Could Have Been Better Today?

_____
_____
_____

Positive Thought Of The Day & Looking Forward

_____
_____
_____

Notes & Reminders

Quote of the Day

As soon as you trust yourself, you will know how to live.
Johann Wolfgang von Goethe

Good Morning Beautiful Soul!

How Do You Feel This Morning?

_____
_____
_____

What Would You Like To Achieve Today?

_____
_____
_____

Accomplishment Aim For The Day:

Guided Imagery: Choose some relaxing meditation music. Use your imagination to transport yourself to a calming, serene place for twenty minutes. After the experience see how you feel and write down the main points of the journey.

_____
_____
_____

How Will You Show Yourself Kindness Today?

_____
_____
_____

Good Evening Beautiful One

Reflections Of The Day

_____

_____

_____

What Did You Achieve Today?

_____

_____

_____

How Do You Feel This Evening?

_____

_____

_____

What Could Have Been Better Today?

_____

_____

_____

Positive Thought Of The Day & Looking Forward

_____

_____

_____

Notes & Reminders

Quote of the Day

Go confidently in the direction of your dreams.
Live the life you've imagined.
Henry David Thoreau

Good Morning Beautiful Soul!

How Do You Feel This Morning?

_____
_____
_____

What Would You Like To Achieve Today?

_____
_____
_____

Accomplishment Aim For The Day:

Clear Your Thoughts: Write down ten thoughts that are bothering you. Then look at each thought and write how you can deal wiith it so it can bring you clarity and peace . Reflect on the way you feel before and after writing.

_____
_____
_____

How Will You Show Yourself Kindness Today?

_____
_____
_____

Good Evening Beautiful One

Reflections Of The Day

_____
_____
_____

What Did You Achieve Today?

_____
_____
_____

How Do You Feel This Evening?

_____
_____
_____

What Could Have Been Better Today?

_____
_____
_____

Positive Thought Of The Day & Looking Forward

_____
_____
_____

Notes & Reminders

DATE:

Quote of the Day

Now faith is the assurance of things hoped for, the conviction of things not seen.
Hebrews 11:1.

Good Morning Beautiful Soul!

How Do You Feel This Morning?

_____
_____
_____

What Would You Like To Achieve Today?

_____
_____
_____

Accomplishment Aim For The Day:

Deep In Thought: Find a piece of writing, it can be a poem, or lyrics that move you and express your current emotions. Write about how it made you feel.

_____
_____
_____

How Will You Show Yourself Kindness Today?

_____
_____
_____

Good Evening Beautiful One

Reflections Of The Day

_____
_____
_____

What Did You Achieve Today?

_____
_____
_____

How Do You Feel This Evening?

_____
_____
_____

What Could Have Been Better Today?

_____
_____
_____

Positive Thought Of The Day & Looking Forward

_____
_____
_____

Notes & Reminders

Quote of the Day

The journey, not the arrival matters.
T.S. Eliot

Good Morning Beautiful Soul!

How Do You Feel This Morning?

What Would You Like To Achieve Today?

Accomplishment Aim For The Day:

Soul Purpose: Consider your soul purpose in this world. Do you feel you are doing what your true calling is? What steps can you take to discover your reason for being on the planet? Write about it.

How Will You Show Yourself Kindness Today?

Good Evening Beautiful One

Reflections Of The Day

_____

_____

_____

What Did You Achieve Today?

_____

_____

_____

How Do You Feel This Evening?

_____

_____

_____

What Could Have Been Better Today?

_____

_____

_____

Positive Thought Of The Day & Looking Forward

_____

_____

_____

Notes & Reminders

Quote of the Day

If you surrendered to the air, you could ride it.
Toni Morrison, Song of Solomon

Good Morning Beautiful Soul!

How Do You Feel This Morning?

_____

_____

_____

What Would You Like To Achieve Today?

_____

_____

_____

Accomplishment Aim For The Day:

Singing: Explore the therapeutic effects of singing. Choose five songs that you love and find the lyrics that most appeal to you focusing on how each song makes you feel.

_____

_____

_____

How Will You Show Yourself Kindness Today?

_____

_____

_____

Good Evening Beautiful One

Reflections Of The Day

_____

_____

_____

What Did You Achieve Today?

_____

_____

_____

How Do You Feel This Evening?

_____

_____

_____

What Could Have Been Better Today?

_____

_____

_____

Positive Thought Of The Day & Looking Forward

_____

_____

_____

Notes & Reminders

Quote of the Day

Change your thoughts and you change your world.
Norman Vincent Peale

Good Morning Beautiful Soul!

How Do You Feel This Morning?

What Would You Like To Achieve Today?

Accomplishment Aim For The Day:

Pamper Your Mind, Body, Spirit: Have a spa day at home with a shower/bath, body scrub, relaxing oils., music, food. Do whatever you find relaxes you. Focus your attention on caring for your whole being. Write after the experience, how it made a difference to your mood reflecting on the before and after.

How Will You Show Yourself Kindness Today?

Good Evening Beautiful One

Reflections Of The Day

_____

_____

_____

What Did You Achieve Today?

_____

_____

_____

How Do You Feel This Evening?

_____

_____

_____

What Could Have Been Better Today?

_____

_____

_____

Positive Thought Of The Day & Looking Forward

_____

_____

_____

Notes & Reminders

Quote of the Day

The best preparation for tomorrow is doing your best today.
H. Jackson Brown Jr.

Good Morning Beautiful Soul!

How Do You Feel This Morning?

_____

_____

_____

What Would You Like To Achieve Today?

_____

_____

_____

Accomplishment Aim For The Day:

Starting Your Self Care Journey: What can you do today to begin to take better care of yourself? Write down as many examples as you can think of and have a daily plan drawn up for the next forty days.

_____

_____

_____

How Will You Show Yourself Kindness Today?

_____

_____

_____

Good Evening Beautiful One

Reflections Of The Day

_____
_____
_____

What Did You Achieve Today?

_____
_____
_____

How Do You Feel This Evening?

_____
_____
_____

What Could Have Been Better Today?

_____
_____
_____

Positive Thought Of The Day & Looking Forward

_____
_____
_____

Notes & Reminders

DATE:

Quote of the Day

Being deeply loved by someone gives you strength, while loving someone deeply gives you courage.
Lao Tzu

Good Morning Beautiful Soul!

How Do You Feel This Morning?

What Would You Like To Achieve Today?

Accomplishment Aim For The Day:

Sunrise Sunset Moments: For one week wake up earlier to see the sunrise and in the evening make time to watch the sunset of the day. Make notes of how it feels to see these wonders of nature.

How Will You Show Yourself Kindness Today?

Good Evening Beautiful One

Reflections Of The Day

_____
_____
_____

What Did You Achieve Today?

_____
_____
_____

How Do You Feel This Evening?

_____
_____
_____

What Could Have Been Better Today?

_____
_____
_____

Positive Thought Of The Day & Looking Forward

_____
_____
_____

Notes & Reminders

Quote of the Day

You will face many defeats in life, but never let yourself be defeated.
Maya Angelou

Good Morning Beautiful Soul!

How Do You Feel This Morning?

_____

_____

_____

What Would You Like To Achieve Today?

_____

_____

_____

Accomplishment Aim For The Day:

Letter To The World: Write a letter that you could read on a platform to the world. Share with the people of the world, your hopes, dreams, what you would like to see happening to make the world a better place. Record your message.

_____

_____

_____

How Will You Show Yourself Kindness Today?

_____

_____

_____

Good Evening Beautiful One

Reflections Of The Day

_____

_____

_____

What Did You Achieve Today?

_____

_____

_____

How Do You Feel This Evening?

_____

_____

_____

What Could Have Been Better Today?

_____

_____

_____

Positive Thought Of The Day & Looking Forward

_____

_____

_____

Notes & Reminders

Quote of the Day

Don't count the days, make the days count.
Muhammad Ali

Good Morning Beautiful Soul!

How Do You Feel This Morning?

_____

_____

_____

What Would You Like To Achieve Today?

_____

_____

_____

Accomplishment Aim For The Day:

Self Compassion: Write yourself some kind, understanding, words of comfort. Let your heart know that you care about yourself, be gentle always.

_____

_____

_____

How Will You Show Yourself Kindness Today?

_____

_____

_____

Good Evening Beautiful One

Reflections Of The Day

_____
_____
_____

What Did You Achieve Today?

_____
_____
_____

How Do You Feel This Evening?

_____
_____
_____

What Could Have Been Better Today?

_____
_____
_____

Positive Thought Of The Day & Looking Forward

_____
_____
_____

Notes & Reminders

Quote of the Day

Keep your face always toward the sunshine and shadows will fall behind you.
Walt Whitman

Good Morning Beautiful Soul!

How Do You Feel This Morning?

What Would You Like To Achieve Today?

Accomplishment Aim For The Day:

Forgiveness: Write down five things that you have done that you have regretted and one by one take a deep breath and forgive yourself and let the memory go.

How Will You Show Yourself Kindness Today?

Good Evening Beautiful One

Reflections Of The Day

_____
_____
_____

What Did You Achieve Today?

_____
_____
_____

How Do You Feel This Evening?

_____
_____
_____

What Could Have Been Better Today?

_____
_____
_____

Positive Thought Of The Day & Looking Forward

_____
_____
_____

Notes & Reminders

Quote of the Day

Act as if what you do makes a difference. It does.
William James

Good Morning Beautiful Soul!

How Do You Feel This Morning?

_____
_____
_____

What Would You Like To Achieve Today?

_____
_____
_____

Accomplishment Aim For The Day:

Awakening Walk: Go for a walk and focus on each of your senses one by one.
Write about how you felt and what you noticed about your surroundings.

_____
_____
_____

How Will You Show Yourself Kindness Today?

_____
_____
_____

Good Evening Beautiful One

Reflections Of The Day

_____

_____

_____

What Did You Achieve Today?

_____

_____

_____

How Do You Feel This Evening?

_____

_____

_____

What Could Have Been Better Today?

_____

_____

_____

Positive Thought Of The Day & Looking Forward

_____

_____

_____

Notes & Reminders

Quote of the Day

Let go or be dragged.
Zen Proverb

Good Morning Beautiful Soul!

How Do You Feel This Morning?

_____

_____

_____

What Would You Like To Achieve Today?

_____

_____

_____

Accomplishment Aim For The Day:

Try a New Recipe: Cook a meal you've never made before from another part of the world and reflect on the experience of learning and tasting something new.

_____

_____

_____

How Will You Show Yourself Kindness Today?

_____

_____

_____

Good Evening Beautiful One

Reflections Of The Day

_____

_____

_____

What Did You Achieve Today?

_____

_____

_____

How Do You Feel This Evening?

_____

_____

_____

What Could Have Been Better Today?

_____

_____

_____

Positive Thought Of The Day & Looking Forward

_____

_____

_____

Notes & Reminders

DATE:

Quote of the Day

There are always flowers for those who want to see them.
Henri Matisse

Good Morning Beautiful Soul!

How Do You Feel This Morning?

_____
_____
_____

What Would You Like To Achieve Today?

_____
_____
_____

Accomplishment Aim For The Day:

Video Time: Choose five motivational videos online to watch that you feel are of a positive nature. With each one summarise how you could incorporate the message into your own life.

_____
_____
_____

How Will You Show Yourself Kindness Today?

_____
_____
_____

Good Evening Beautiful One

Reflections Of The Day

_____
_____
_____

What Did You Achieve Today?

_____
_____
_____

How Do You Feel This Evening?

_____
_____
_____

What Could Have Been Better Today?

_____
_____
_____

Positive Thought Of The Day & Looking Forward

_____
_____
_____

Notes & Reminders

Congratulations Amazing Soul

You have completed a wonderful adventure.
Now you begin the real journey of your
rediscovering your reality.

Live, Love & Enjoy Your Beautiful Life.

Love

Mimi Novic